MANDIBLE WISHBONE SOLVENT

PHOENIX POETS

Edited by Srikanth Reddy

Rosa Alacá, Douglas Kearney &

Katie Peterson, consulting editors

Mandible Wishbone Solvent

ASIYA WADUD

THE UNIVERSITY OF CHICAGO PRESS
CHICAGO & LONDON

The University of Chicago Press, Chicago 60637
The University of Chicago Press, Ltd., London
© 2024 by The University of Chicago
All rights reserved. No part of this book may be used or reproduced in any manner whatsoever
without written permission, except in the case of brief quotations in critical articles and reviews.
For more information, contact the University of Chicago Press, 1427 E. 60th St., Chicago, IL 60637.
Published 2024
Printed in the United States of America

33 32 31 30 29 28 27 26 25 24   1 2 3 4 5

ISBN-13: 978-0-226-83095-7 (paper)
ISBN-13: 978-0-226-83096-4 (e-book)
DOI: https://doi.org/10.7208/chicago/9780226830964.001.0001

All artwork and photography by Asiya Wadud except p. 66, *Suspension bridge collapses into the
Tacoma Narrows*, 1940, Tacoma, Washington. Prints and Photographs Division, Library of
Congress, Washington DC, LCCN 2006687436.

Library of Congress Cataloging-in-Publication Data

Names: Wadud, Asiya, author.
Title: Mandible, wishbone, solvent / Asiya Wadud.
Other titles: Phoenix poets.
Description: Chicago : The University of Chicago Press, 2024. | Series: Phoenix poets |
    Includes bibliographical references.
Identifiers: LCCN 2023034990 | ISBN 9780226830957 (paperback) | ISBN 9780226830964 (ebook)
Subjects: LCGFT: Poetry.
Classification: LCC PS3623.A35223 M36 2024 | DDC 811/.6—dc23/eng/20230804
LC record available at https://lccn.loc.gov/2023034990

♾ This paper meets the requirements of ANSI/NISO Z39.48-1992 (Permanence of Paper).

This book is for Howard Smith,
     Black sculptor, printmaker
        and collage artist who
     spent much of his life in Fiskars, Finland

Smith passed away on February 4, 2021.

     His work has been a guiding force these past years.

When you used the carbon paper correctly, you ended up with two copies of the same document. The top white sheet bore original ink handwriting, the bottom white sheet was the mimic of every stroke and dot. What I had not noted at the time was that on the black paper there was a third copy of whatever had been written. The black paper was ridged and marked with all the original handwriting. Black on black, full of meaning, but shaped by absence. The black paper was the ghostly record. Black on black, secretly sensible.

TEJU COLE, Black Paper

CONTENTS

MANDIBLE WISHBONE SOLVENT

PART 1

Other Ovals All Along

#221 ½

       Ochre drifts deliver the oysters
       Reprisal in their opening mouths
       Each expels what it nurtured
Other ovals all along

Onion skin
       parchment
       onion skin fermented
       all cultivated alliums

       ocean drift delivers all umber
       prised from the low tide
gathered up the dispersed objects, made them an offering

Onion skin
       And overture
O and orange peeled
Or singed parchment   O
O or starboard, port O or focal
O or   my
       mother's
       abject
       order
              Other o
              Other o

Zero marks an absence   Hart Island
           Overflow

Effluence onward and grace   O   and
In other languages we'd say, How I missed you
While we place our hands together   O
Other islands with an expendable O

I am solvent, deciduous
Mourning birds nesting   O
In their half-finished homes
      they enter through the Open window
Shelf for their Only songs
An operating theater slips and becomes diction or
      the first night of Ramadan, the cleaved Evensong
      Spectacular in its lament and ordered
      Lone song
Operatic or O
Open against the horizontal seams
    equatorial
      O open frontier or a sieve
      Catchment or a swift return
      Pilgrimage or gilded

An operating theater slips and becomes diction or other futures
      Spectacular in its lament and ordered
      Only song
      Imperative that the song finishes
Let the song finish, then
      sit inside the keening, then   a single hymn for all of them

                    It begins the same way it ends
               with the slipping of the long
                   vowels
              and the shuttering of the others

A rowboat is a manual

As in hand over hand in what
     We sought   O
Soft O like oblong
And original or ordinance and horizon
       Other islands with an expendable O
       The breath we breathe into it

                             O

                         all the hours it takes to articulate
                            the O
                       by the time we finish
                       our mouths are spent
                       days   or
                       hours of   O   work

Now other steady streams build too
       music or grayscale ocean or nautical O
       The drum is taut   O
Since all the sounds ring in order   we
Call it a precision or   song

Later
We place the metronome on the island
       It disregards the place
Keeps up its one dirge

Lets it slip and finds its chorus
We place the instrument at the water's edge
But the pulse builds from the center
     Salt keeps the water lifted   O
anathema
     or anthem
anthem or iron-rich

Rearrange the parchment
Make of it an envelope
Place inside it the soft O

poised in hover hours

the hand
does the
work

my hands   or
a labor of love

or
a labor of dexterous
want

      both hands act in credence
      to work all the palms' grit
      to see what remains
          what remnants the palms insist
          what their lifelines etch
          ragged as these last revenants

      may come as off-kilter
      revelry now and askance

my hands   grazed the work
rested in preparation for

gentle mastery of
deference
      the salt-filmed waters

I touched the velvet-rimmed—
fissured
its autumn, moss-gold pleasure

in a labor
of love

my hands
grazed the blue green algae

I   took care   to remove
what was noxious
but   most   of   all   took
care   not   to   drink   it

skimmed the surface to get
a better look
netted all the algae
the net capitulated to poison
it took the bloom, the burden
it understood the rupture
its descent was threefold—palm oil, lament, still surface
each its own proliferation

in the fresh water
I declared what lack
of buoyancy.   in

              the salt water I fed
              the preservation

or call it the labor
of containment
how every limb
lay lifted
everything in me hovered at the
surface

cupped my hands—hold the
water. cupped hands
creature a tapered fissure

the Camargue hours drift
through the fingers' gaps
the space shows us what
futures

the hand does the
work. I promote its precision—
        the singular fingerprints

cupped at my mouth the
hands now act as colloquial chamber

palm outstretched
is a patient gesture
        a lung's cavity another silent
extension

        all together
        10 fingers

my hands have done a workload
plaster hands fused together
my index fingers meeting
all incremental knowledge
same as the salt water
each minute builds as a choral hour
then hours

my hands didn't touch the
blue-green algae. I know
it's noxious and I didn't want
any trouble

my other hand cups the
Camargue water
I am ambivalent about any
future.
there are more bodies of water

hunger is an
overture
        handed knowledge
a labor of love or   the structured work of want

the hand does
the work
the Camargue presses us
the landscapes rather dividend   saltpeter to say the future
saltpeter to say what preserves us

seven desire lines one map

fillet meets
foil meets
figment.
     filigree fills the   fist

the petal
    will

        silence the dome

                     open and let in the air
              deliver what it offered

                    the cumulus falls
                    froths as its accretion grows at the
                            lattice
                                        or our guesswork

        grain winnows
the petal
the petal
and tenders the dome

what sovereign minute   or dome

features
the furnace?

the petal
        as foreman
forsythia becomes
forensic now
            stills the bell, stills the dome now

disclose concentric centers

miscalculation of moss and ore, sediment that said nine times the rain relented
    yesterday the center vents the center said
velvet as yesterday's portion, the courage to till the toil
let Tuesday rest here
      let Wednesday be a looser burden.

I did peel back the center, let the green flame of it glow, let the blue lantern guide us
      let the acrylic surface dry
       first the sanding, concentric circles condition the wood grain
       come to respect its given logic   come to rest my hands here and clear all
        the deadwood
      the courage to crack the yolk and let the yellow run across my hands, let it
        drench in its soft boil, let its gorge assemble what the rain remits

the withered center dazzled one decade into the future, force stricken, and I read its
    core
the message given was laden, held up by the worn trellis
      the light filtered in through thirty-two even cracks
        set at the core angle.
when I unraveled the center other codes came to exist, each its own logic

could be an orange gleaming yolk, Mount Diablo inside me, the curtain tries to resist
    the breeze
      it settles the space with what's left, nothing else disproven
all impropriety came with its own conditions, dividends in whatever manifestation,
    each a determined quality of its own making
every vessel held its own future, every sodden weft and purl

I have made a treaty with eleven ways of seeing, each their own sub-accord,
    credence made by braiding psalms
        each terse amendment held together by seven strands of gold filament. I have
            made each apology slovenly born in yesterdays
        a cylindrical throughway, grief cut lengthwise then done
        I have made peace with the allocation   courted in trim weeks
            the green frailty
         luxury comes by will or creed, take a chisel in every hand and work, suf-
            fused to all the logic

it was easy, the thrill came in a book of corrugated verse
        seven housed in a city block
between them grew the simulacra of pine trees
        a tender rendition extended the whole forest down to every splayed leaf
        the leaden the leached—each limb of each tree supplication and dripped in
            the choral yesterdays

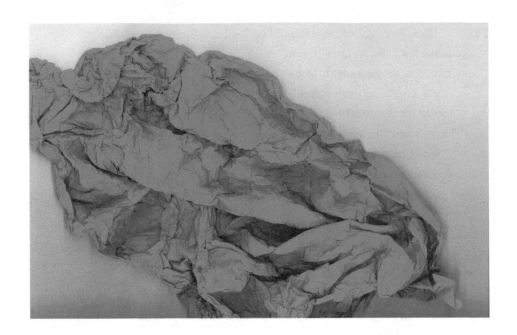

the herring arrive as overture

bay space
fastened to any
          extruded
      surface

                  a leeway
            courses the spine of the island
            gray nodules mark the keening distance
                  ligature or implied latitude
                  latitude or pin grenade
            pine grain or hand grenade

how clinical their   movement
how fine their sutures how ready their scriptures
then shunt them

sculptural or   holy book
receding inlet
withheld in covenant   in credence

                  it is monastic to wrestle the burden
                  monastic to wring them
                  the herring arrive as overture
                  and quicksilver
                  their dirge a shoal they make
                  their oil and feed, near supplicants

let me, mere time
leaden water
solemn or not   silver or not
provocation in the knotted and brutal
by brutal I mean crushed
by

the load
         of the
      aggregate songbirds
crushed by the load
of the agate burdens
      crushed by the little me
      the metal me
leaking dispersal
the newsprint
the logic foretold
through inlet

we scooped the water
crystal in kindness
in clarity the
breath in constant surrender
took me for a nation
breathing so even
took all my continent's drift
      forced me to eat it
      forced me inside it
          where I slept all winter
          birdlike and nested
      abdicated to nothing
objected only to havens built
in my metabolic absence
aseptic and needling still loveless
dry land but muted

little inlet guide my distance
my careful hand
my right hand
and meandering character
my dissonance
thread bear and canter   the kingdom and silence

bay space gives way to
tame inlet to
prayer and cusp of belief
wrought island
        unholy becomes riven
by proximal creed

the leeway
lurking, taut against
line or latitude
sutures or sculpture or holy book
        do the work to ferry the movement
        a prayer but still muted
        invitational cobalt in that the
        altar radiates all transient antecedents

let's be the blue
object, abdicate to nothing
grieving the gray line
all the same, forgave the twilight
the flash of evening
what distance   what distance
and furrowed   disturbance

elocutions   startle then slip
steady now   steady now   let me now

all excess bloomed then felled

all the verdant decay while looking at the mountain
the room locks from the outside
                        from the inside it's tame
a tangle unfolds under the guise of reverence and three church bells
for convenience let's call it a way of dying
        let's call it shatterproof or resistance
the narrows bred their own heroes
the rest was cellular

all verdant decay while inside the mountain
                        near the peak
the pit leaves a hum, then decay brick by brick
I am tenfold of logic then hum then buttress and inside

I am done with decadence and condolence and that was easy
        shed the vessels at the right angle
ninety degrees does its namesake does its blame
                        viscous in the closets and vicious at the bedsides

black logic runs through the tobacco leaf and the island
obsidian is temporal and the tent is full already so don't rest yet or ask after the
    tangier's nest
                don't ask after why you didn't call
a decade passes in four days
my logic of time remains abhorrent decay does its work
        doves fall from the left frame
        gems and lateral logic souvenirs and that was also life

the room locks from the outside from the inside it's tame
a tangle unfolds under the guise of revelry we have been here before
a bouquet of roses petal by petal against the porcelain floors

the island builds a structure to fortify the closets
                    the doors open outward trying to receive us
doors revolve and create the vacuum and concealer or covenant hidden in
    the fine print

let's call it alone or compline because the mountain finally moved all visions
    doubled
        apparitions pierced and threaded red-raw and glistening
a series of hhhhh   as ahhhh   as heave
as shhhh   and shame   as half as lowly more covenant
hhhhh more cove

I am forlorn walloped by my own fading memory that stills me shrill logic at the cell
level then some. I am forlorn free from history or at least souvenirs and doves in my
left hand I move them to my right hand they sleep all along align the timbers and let
them speak

I am a paring knife, all violences betrothed to me in a dream last Sunday. My tongue
knotted and tied—red ribbon at the uvula
why bother to speak when the creed is a shorn ribbon tattered and wayward?

all the marrow was yesterday's meal and marrow is yesterday's meal in that it hinges
the bones—burrows in black space and makes a pendulum. I am a pendulum—
tobacco fields shack prayer beads so weighted they ascend because what else?
a rosary bleeds in place of me

I am all premature violences set inside the mountain
I didn't leave it all alone
I fell inside the forest then became the ring and let the ring become me

every loss is a ring further around the tree, a noose that gives way to gravity then
no matter the age it gives loose to grammar and the frame and I am done with the
narrows the ribbon shorn and tattered and the bones sinking into their meager
cartilage trying to bear the burden, bear December and me

I have locked heaven inside a thimble—it is meager so it was easy bitterfruit so it
breaded at the slightest mention of oil. I am a haven in December. The thread is
woven gold for courage and sixteen was threadbare anyway. I let the bitterfruit live in
me in my earth's last cavity laden with loose grammar, every ring then every ring then

every night eludes me in that cellular or leavened is better on the body
all mutable violence of country and creed made to resist
any shadow made a fallacy of future logic unknotted
tongue, please speak to me—prayer at compline suffused in my last bones
gravity has already made a port wherein enters all fluid—heaven or inferno
    rests in limbo

all excess bloomed in the mouth cut
vertically then the knife exacts the bloomed excess
from bone leaking excess fallacy loose grammar
earth's last cavity every night eludes me

      rest
      now
    may you be among the animals the
    animals who levitate as soon as gravity speaks
    its name
    gravity succumbs to fire to new grass
    plumed boats to eighty

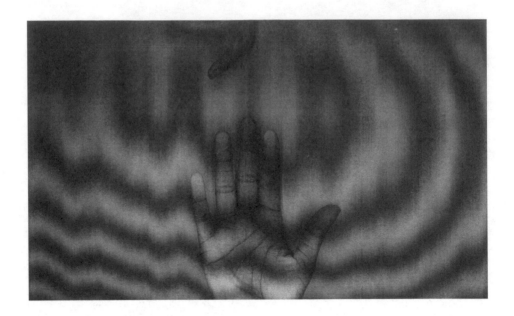

and green waters and green

One more year of gray friction at the
broken mountain   feet wearing their soft forgiveness
nestled by the green water cotton picked clean and cuffed the rising algae

and one looped year near the mountain   trick the eye at the peak
      soon tactile becomes an only rhythm, index fingers all ornamental
let them slip between my trussed teeth
        inside the mouth or complete covenant, trellis and a lattice wrapped
concrete laid to keep the ground cover cooler near the mountain, let the ground
    cover in my mouth
           just a way to say relief from the heat, next best thing to a shade tree
crumbling anchors used to suffuse then disperse all the mountain's agency
laid the bricks in a forty-brick row then started three bricks deep near the last years
      scant way up
     it gets aaaaaa at the mountain
        homage to the plaintive years at the spire
        feet with a soft song

let it rest in the left hand or passes for the left hand or passes for the left hand
    let it rest on the bricks laid or crimped anchors laid or trick the eye then the eye
let it ease up and slide across and be so tamed and green water and green water and green

be a bridge over something
for Howard Smith

be a bridge over something

      be echo or residue or green question

be a loose suture, extension and supplement be a primrose and covenant

     be an image pinched and pruned turned oblong
          hemmed
              and hemmed
         and let go

be a bridge over   echo the dense ocean
      make the water rise and let go the road rimmed with each obstacle

be the seventeenth hour
      hovered at the door then tinned ocean
that dreams echo and bridge and
suspension

be here then   a footpath that brims   encase canals and obstacles

be the shake the slipslap breathe the breath that lets you in
     breathe the breath that railed   dense echo
O   dense echo, throw me seven more stitched hems   I will sink in

1.2

after *Motionless Dancers* by Howard Smith

the twinned emblems
     eschew the opening
opt for the fortress
unraveling then   weave

twinned to say mirrored reflexive

archipelago or tamed or a subtlety
     all fortunes
curved the long way

hunger ensues
     begins with the diadem
     ends with the aperture
             not prophetic but
let the moths live
they have already nested

     took kingdom
    the diadem folds along its natural seam

PART 2

Scant Excess Enclosed in a Film

Mandible Wishbone Solvent
after *Oracle/Hero* by Howard Smith

roped in incremental ghost tens
      future tens clairvoyant tens   home tens

blue slips beneath the exposed wing
tilt then seam then an angle spent all inside
the distance between thumb and thimble and fingerprint

      height exceeds then brims
      makes a solvent of it

       what vaunted green excess enclosed in each skimmed year then the years
           vanquished any fuchsia sky
      the excess leaking forward filmed aqua
               filled aqua

fastened by ulna by increments of ten
fortunes sidled with
what have we when we give the mandible the fragments by
  tens?
tender tilt at ninety degrees to unearth
blue slips beneath the exposed wing
  continents
  contain
  futures
you
  be here

      you
        be here tender tilt
        remiss in skies
        scant excess enclosed in a film that gives more than
        brimmed solvents to wrest time

Shorn, treaded, red
after *Satellites 27* by Etel Adnan

ochre starts
       commence   catalyst and evensong enters

a flame lit arched and yearn
gleam, twofold

weary but not from this life
in time flame begets pools of
shorn Decembers
limber months evade us
       the flood
          begets
               burnished

catalyst and a hem
treaded red, quaked

slide gleam and slide trifold
       mirroring the fresh lake whirring
mirroring the whirring shorn wave

eleven nocturnes
       you Fibonacci
you catacomb

a symmetrical open plane, curve
after *Untitled, 2018* by Etel Adnan

early embers
       deluge
slim still

       ascendant still
caution
     or I am still

calcium verdant
      logic

a threaded needle disciplined
a threaded needle carves a field
     I am laden with early embers
     letting them encase me

the arch of a blue chord
     skims
changed ember charged
     slope up the bedrock
slope up the decay up the casement
up the caution up the frame

In the checkpoint I was all arms / all face
after *Glaring* by Ben Krusling

what animal and burdens
      me with its own barren heart
baronesses to wonder then the
upstream so the upstream

      time and again I have held the wilted photograph to my face to smell it
      make of it an arrangement then bouquet, cursed it or cruised through
let the time orient the justice
the precipice then court it

the cattle prod is a discipline in a night stick or anathema disciple in heaven can wait
jurisdiction or redlined or heaven can wait

all my palm-bearing witnesses or replete with a witch window left open
           to gain a vantage of the field which I lay with seeds and ruin

hemmed up inside the seeds were
the witnesses, white-knuckled
and clawing at the fixtures
by the ceiling. cawing then a gentle forgiveness governs me
laid bare the jurisdiction, ten years at a time

all dare to climb the column and lie in wait
laced and lurked and comforted by the hinge of attrition meets monument meets
facsimile

I am no longer burdened by anything with the black mark or the
    black mark
    let its insides speak as organ and filament, lace or lattice

let it spill out the gapped seam, zippered but still reckless
forlorn and roughcut, a pennant in the end

    the striation in the leaf is its own leverage so
I am not governed by the island or the island in me
mired by the island or the island in me
or the distance always made me a shrill line
more sudden than the long gaze to anything
        this could be one future

the day spills its own accord then
breaches the levy then the lake drained
all lakes breach the levy and the lake drains
 a monument rests at the bottom of the grate:
 memorial to still life still thimble-filled stillness
 and placed as a coda or footnote or secretion

I am a green leaf, disciple of chlorophyll
round robin of green leaf—dim the planter and the water
       drain the lake region then the gutters

a surge comes when it comes
every state builds a retaining wall a wailing wall
or a scrim. everyone builds the scrim

 a sieve that lets the water in when it comes
 lets the trickle trout through to let it breathe

drain the alkaline lake and watch the retaining wall
    let the load meant to bear it bear the load, see how the retaining wall bends
        swerves and genuflects

        or the alkaline lake hovers back at the bottom all use spent acid rises to the
            surface, hinged

    or the plastics hover at the bottom all use spent acids resist the hinge

the disc takes shape, dear cutlass
after Sara Haq's *Things I did that nobody noticed (but that changed everything)*

how does umber talk back? breach the cliff. spill the cleft

    noiseless distance
filaments then reach
humble in aptitude
      padding about their velvet movement

the thin strip sought
     a series of mauve questions—inlaid or a reed

all featherweight beginnings carried in
the construction
a brute structure
pinpricked and let it rise

the modulation of the stream, a canter
master of its own signal   eye to the
                         needle

      I have brought my blunt rhythms
      blades that don't require sharpening, mauve
      blades that act like a widening penumbra, mauve
      acuity or commitment

everything streams like clockwork
the muscular threads hard-won
the buoyancy is a reminder
elasticity its own kingdom
the buoyancy is an imprint
buoyancy all through the garden
every tool streams like clockwork
our chronic condition is   sit with this

                                        all islands form their own urgent net worth

the disc takes shape
dear cutlass
the discus or obelisk
obsidian—mourn
black as in   all tints reaching and the   vale to loop

                                    I have found a way worthy in

carved a clean column—an easement, extending through the threshold

I knew nothing of the cellar walls
        the pavement
        constructs its own cloister
anything bears the brunt, the burden
the urgency bears it
the brutalists do too

        every obelisk is its own inheritance
        remnants of all other discs, my anthem

delirium
    quickness and tender   all horizon and broad channel
                                                 the discs still in discovery
                                                 constellations still askew

now, I have thought to eviscerate all objects mauve
to see what they hold in ligature in signage
to grasp what they need for the attenuation
what could be our just architecture

                all hues resting in arrangement
                nestled gently, in kin
                entangled as the lines straighten
                estrangement is not a given

I have outlined in red all my wayworthiness in
we have equally shared the burden
I have made a home that contains us
and the stockpile of houses
        —all the ways to say blue
        and how the heat encases us

all this time as tactile object
the days passing like a taciturn word
the minutes even smaller
every day encases the given hours
how they consecrate the whip stitch

all lake beds
diminutive subjects against the poured concrete

           the gray blade—the point projects
           all my discrete futures
           all the unhinged fathomings
           their noble waiting

      one collection speaks to our marigold filling—every pistil held
      sun-fold or leached or blooming
      the reasons obscured, or simply they have their own existence
darkness consecrates one more darkroom
throbbing in its own center

how I examined the roots, took measure
methods that came in a long dream
starlings in their long division
all the ancillary roots forming deltas
a thick lattice then root work
each cast in infused blues

acid engraves the cutlass
extrudes the point of the blade
lingered at the lintel

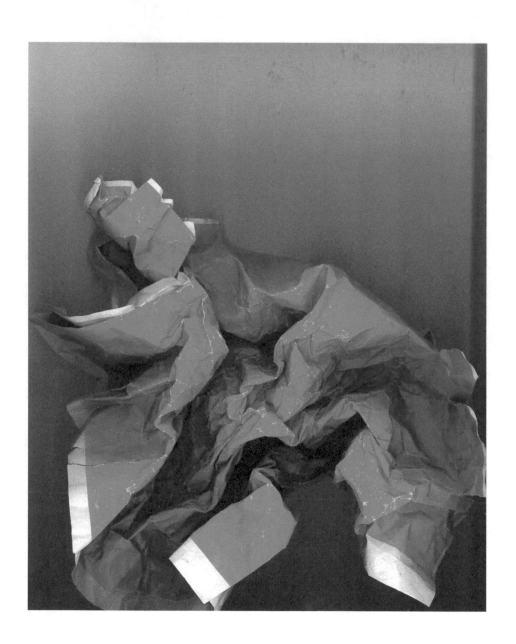

PART 3

Microplane Weights / Accounts of First Contact

cobalt mirror image 1

lengthen the lintel or lean by the marigold   cable
christened threads
        or image
winnowed or drifted
grafted at the
        christened
            drift

then each shoulder drapes the new lintel
slides from clavicle to shoulder girdle
        scapula
all the while
        marigold and nectar
            corn silk
canary
        lengthen the lintel or lean by the   cable

cobalt mirror image 2

a range of blue sounds or chamber room
      draped
by
a stack of cement bricks
or corner
stills the space
      by weight or grip

      history or four corners take the room

continual whir or slip
      makes an environment for shaft or shunt the drift
      shunted into a smaller space

interior and keep moving in—then

cobalt mirror image 3

I wanted to hear all manner of bow meets thrill
        glass curl and my hand, a magnet
the bell
        the timber
the green tonic
        silent gold shadows or
        mourn us

        great green ghosts fill up the corner then move in

        green ghosts fill up the
                        interior and keep moving in then

the space holds my hand, held me then

thin—or the mirage upon mylar—sliver of continuous momentum

                all my life I have had just one
                body
                it thrills me to watch my life through one dark lens, then

thrills me to become the carrier wind then hold it

black space cumbersome against the bow's long hum and diction
black asphalt against again
black heat or green ghosts begin the journey then

the cement blocks are still where they are
        they have not moved since
        we took great honor in placing them by the marigold
marked the acute urgent noon with a hum
        then shadow

cobalt mirror image 4

we could meet by twos or threes bear witness
to each other
        hands fit for the slow supplicant
I am wishing and dawn and dawn and dawn

                        the blank space relents

the black pockets get filled
the back pockets get filled then

long shadows or lore
a shadow box ultimately
        soft work and

battalion of one feels so lost and peaceful
        holes and a mess at the very least
                draped or high finish
bore barren
                bore kindred

cobalt mirror image 5

        I have let go of constraints and
summer—honed and humming
tinned and sinkhole

virtue or hemmed in
      all fair and faint
filling up what virtue remains

emptied then all detriment the
surface matte and growing matter

cobalt mirror image 6

parenthetical whisper
disperse
whispers

conveyance sonic grace

tiptoe into the water
microplane weights

    accounts of first contact
    an accord made in good faith

Fibonacci follows me as a gesticulation as a framework continual shift of expectation
align the weight
    mass
    form   flow

green wind makes of me a
loose new bouquet   or a mile
milled wind makes the manner
the vessels
                    within
                    the chambers the
                    low light lies

take a corner
		double it or transitive
		reflective or parenthetical
	hemmed in by the hum
vested by the selvage
by the vessel

my mind makes for me a window then a door

makes for me marrow or an inside filament
figment or sepulcher sculpture monument or inside cave

slips of windowpanes—yawning at the seams
      or permanent fixture green lathe or marrow or nested

          an interior door ajar though mesh so more sieve than door nest of open win-
               dows does the mesh make

               a structured or strident city grid meets girth meets exurb
               the monument makes for me a relic or fixture a fixture then plaque
               gilded and scapula, evergreen aseptic gaps could the flowers make

my mange makes for me a dinner, softened inside any gilded mouth
      mostly cavity or crown
      bridge or gully
      a monument to marrow and what runs inside it, oxygen to further a future

                              stove top or otherwise
                               step inside or at the hem

my manager gathers the marriage of order of alliums and almost and
soft cells and tender and tender and strident the window

my mind makes for me marrow or filigree
the intricacies delivered by the minute
the marrow creates and feeds a steady stream
both a summer and a selfless season

silent or apparition or the noise could speak

all brackish and woven
warp weft and still life
each a degree of the aperture

my mind makes for me a thin, tame vine
settling into its tangled rope
woven up inside the cavernous glass tubes
climbing up the facade
then inside through a pitched roof window
what work
what worth

my mind makes for me a window,
    brushstroke, or way out
scraping back gold filament
door or otherwise a fixture or otherwise filmed futures

PART 4

The Shroud Can Encase Whatever We Tell It

Nearly Any Two Things Can Cohere

> There is no chance that we will fall apart
> There is no chance
> There are no parts.
>
> JUNE JORDAN, "Poem Number Two on Bell's Theorem,
> or the New Physicality of Long Distance Love"

1. Imagine a Condition of Ongoing Want,[1] an Isthmus Condition

The condition of most of our lives is that of continuous flight, in some manner or form—flight from faulty logic, from place of birth to the place we alight, from situations that no longer serve us, from political precarity. Flight, as in rupture. The isthmus is the gabled structure that supports flight. It is the decent gangway, the patient tunnel. The corridor that was already named. The allée with its payarded trees, spilling out onto the slick boulevard. The muted alley. The juncture. Guidelines, or artery. A radiant, focused under passage. Imagine many minor points of transit, unified in their relative liminality, betwixt & between, two brevities, humbled relative nothingnesses, their algaed stepping stone, their insignificance, their transitory nature.

An isthmus connects two distinct and otherwise separate land masses. It is necessary, connective tissue, latticework that renders two unequivocated topographies part of a single larger one, forming a reverberation. It resounds, hums. The isthmus, by nature of its role as threadbare lattice, animates the possible similarities between two places while tamping the mounting distance. No matter the attenuation of the thin, long space between, the isthmus is a commitment in the landform, a promise that transit ends. It is a topography that notes a yoking but also one that ultimately disgorges, then delivers.

Embedded in the isthmus is the electric transit. And transit through the isthmus may be difficult—nearly impossible—but perhaps we can quell its anxiety and terror because etched onto the landform is an end to the journey. *Isthmus* means transit in Greek. By nature and topography, it is liminal, bound on both ends by concrete, firm land. The masses that connect one end to another are generally bigger, more expansive, with a more notable imprint than the narrow

---

1   "We as human beings are not only able to imagine a condition of ongoing want, but are also able to maintain this condition of want and moreover to call it life." Inger Christensen, *The Conditions of Secrecy: Selected Essays* (New York: New Directions, 2018), 78.

strip of the isthmus itself. We can see this by looking at the map. We can look at the Isthmus of Panama or the Isthmus of Tehuantepec in southern Mexico, or the Karelian Isthmus at the edges of land between Finland and Russia. But what if we acknowledge that the etch of the isthmus is an equal or heavier burden than what rests on either end, that sometimes the transit is the defining character of the events on either side?

‡ ‡ ‡

An isthmus is a passageway, threshold, underbrush, thicket, and deliverance. It is to funnel. To chart. It is a throughway. A shunt, a directive. The isthmus can assuage fear because we hold steady the possibility of what awaits us on the other side.

The myopia of an isthmus can curry a claustrophobia, as everything that once had plenty of space for movement is now funneled through a narrowing expanse. It is siphoned through a winnowing enclosure. But maybe it is also an opportunity to slough off what is of diminishing significance, at least during passage itself.

2. Body

Yesterday I watched a short clip on the Human Rights Watch Twitter feed. In it, ten two-gallon jugs of water sat lined up in a stretch of the Sonoran Desert, right where the US and Mexico meet. With calculation and deliberate action, a US Customs and Border Protection agent picked up a full container and drained it of its contents. He drained another, and although the clip ended after he did so, I can only assume that he continued emptying them all. The water had been left by members of No More Deaths, a border-action organization, and were meant to offer reprieve to those making the journey from Central America onward to the United States. The border agent presumably lifted ten separate containers and emptied each. Depending on how you look at it, that was either ten separate decisions, or a single, yoked one. Maybe it was barely a decision at all, removed of its vitriol, scrubbed clean, now a simple muscle memory of an act that once contained vitriol, but now the bridge that connects this action to actual people suffering at this crossing no longer exists.

What do we envision when we imagine the journey of someone, now arm's length from the southern US border? How can we become capacious in our rendering of the journey itself, generous enough to regard the full latitude of the isthmus? Can we try to envision the field of decisions that it took to decide to leave? Imagine leaving your own house, the place where you live. In the kitchen, there are your pots and pans, your towels hang in the bathroom, maybe there are fresh sheets on the bed. Maybe the weather is finally turning, and you cracked open the window when you return home from work, the work that provides your sustenance. Each act represents a small decision that, fastened together, makes up your life, a small shield from the world at large, a vestibule.

To leave your home, you start walking, and you continue walking, and there is all the weight borne in that walking. Perhaps you set out to travel a certain number of hours, and halfway through the day, the only thing you can consider is the heaviness of the load and the weight that leaving bears. Blisters are forming on your heels; you weren't able to say goodbye to an old neighbor whom you have known forever; you are questioning whether the meager items you took with you are going to be enough until your next point of reprieve.

If we cannot imagine a destitute journey, one born in an urgency that forces someone to voyage across borders, then it is in that moment that it is possible to empty water from jugs, again and again.

3. A Point on the Map

What do we envision when we hear the name of a point on a map? What clear images take shape when we hear of a point of departure and then its connective point, and how do the images transform each time a different connective point is held in relation to that point of origin? There is Tegucigalpa, for example. Have you ever been? What develops in the momentary tension between the time we hear the name Tegucigalpa and Dallas, Texas? If we have never been to the capital city of Honduras, we may have ready a set of impressions to rely upon, filling in a place that would otherwise remain vacant. We may rely on rote, distorted images to fill the void. The pictures get shunted along, affirmed in their propulsion, in their ability to help make meaning of a place, to give it resonance. Or it may remain a blank slate for us, simply a name of a place where we will never travel and where we do not know a single soul. Maybe, for some, Tegucigalpa conjures no feeling—animus, warmth, or otherwise. And if it conjures nothing, perhaps it is easier to empty the bottles of water left for thirsty people at the border. The images we form of a place and of a state get shunted along, and they give credence to whatever we need to believe.

You begin the journey with the expectation that the topography and landscape enact the manner in which they've been inscribed on the map. But borders always shift, and it is possible that, before your journey ends, the borders will have shifted around you. You have done nothing different. The external forces shifted around you, against you, in fact, in retaliation to you. They lash out as a way to show you that a border will always be mutable and that, if you're not wanted, the range and scope of the isthmus will simply change at will.

An isthmus is a manifestation of our directed focus—it encases all our propulsive desire. Its focus propels us, creating a new field of vision. I came across an article documenting some firsthand accounts of families making the journey from Central America to the United States, in what's been deemed the Migrant Caravan. In one story Ani Alvarado from Comayagua, Honduras, notes that she "get[s] used to whatever," that she "learned from life."[2] Maybe she knows exactly what it means for a border to shift around her, to start cobbling together something different than what existed when she imagined the other side of the isthmus.

4. Ligature

If you live inside the brackishness of two spaces, the chronically, committedly, critically in-between, perhaps embedded in you is an animated vitality, a feeling that change is always possible, that change is imminent.

Last summer I went to Riga, Latvia, in search of a place to feel alone and small—small in relation to the colossal scale of Soviet-era architecture, where the built environment speaks to a not-so-distant political ideology. I wonder how these architectural remnants assert themselves and how—if at all—their daily use and vitality are collectively reimagined once their ideological use is spent. I became enamored of a particular building situated on Valguma Street, though now I understand there are several like it in Riga.

2   Kirk Semple and Todd Heisler, "Caravan Walks Quietly On, U.S. Opposition a Distant Rumble," *New York Times*, November 9, 2018.

I can't speak to the interior of this building. I only snapped a picture of its blocky isthmus en route to meet a friend's friend. A transverse section hangs over the street traffic passing beneath it, and it joins two buildings, or perhaps is a portion of one building held aloft, its middle structure raised. I can't say if each of the four rows of five windows constitute a single apartment or if the inhabited space extends into the masses at either side. I wonder about this connective strait exactly because it does not appear to be a point of transit at all. It is habitation in bifurcation, resident above the road; those inside etch a longitudinal insistence in their steady state and daylong coming and going. Perhaps if you live in the isthmus, you live committed to coming and going.

‡   ‡   ‡

And what about bridges? A bridge connects two disparate fields, much like an isthmus. It assumes a just union, the supposition made manifest and apparent. Bridges—physical bridges and bridge notions—also collapse, setting loose two ideas that once gripped each other, sending them into freefall, a disassociation. The two formerly coupled notions no longer connect. On July 1, 1940, the Tacoma Narrows Bridge, which connected Tacoma and Kitsap Peninsula in Washington state, opened to the public, and a little over four months later, it violently collapsed into Puget Sound. For about four months, two landforms previously unbound were held in accord.

Suspension bridge collapses into the Tacoma Narrows, 1940,
Tacoma, Washington. Prints and Photographs Division,
Library of Congress, Washington DC, LCCN 2006687436.

If your first encounter with the Tacoma Narrows strait was sometime between the collapse of the bridge and its eventual rebuilding in 1950, you may have been unaware that a bridge once fixed these two landmasses together. What changes in the moment that this knowledge is made known to us? How does it redraw the periphery of the map in our minds?

5. Nearly Any Two Things Can Cohere

In the landform on the map, we know an isthmus is an isthmus because when we look to its diagram, we see its definitive structure—a relative largeness, the narrower strip, another something larger. We connect these three discrete forms because we witness their readymade coherence. All we have to do is follow the summary of logic already laid bare. Other times the possible isthmus of landform and logic is obfuscated; it rests in a state of possible coherence.

About a year ago, I rode the A train from my house in Bed Stuy to the Upper West Side, where I was taking a four-week class on morality and mysticism in Clarice Lispector's work. I settled into my seat. As a woman, I am conditioned to train my eyes, to take in everything within my purview, and then that which might enter it. What might enter—affixing one moment to the next—hangs in the balance, awaiting a possible coherence. A man entered the subway car and stalked down the aisle. He fixed his attention on a person across from me and then, despite many empty seats, sat beside her. He got close to her face. I couldn't hear what he was saying, but his body language was menacing, and so close, without reservation. For the entire sixty seconds or so of this closeness, she fixed her gaze out the window, hands clasped in her lap. She was so unchanging in posture that I might not have believed the man was there at all. The only indication she had felt his presence came later, at the next stop when he got off; she stretched her legs across three seats facing her and put her bag in a fourth, warding off any more approachments.

In the absence of a manifest landscape or logic, there is no way to know that any two moments should be held in relief, bound together. Boarding the train a moment later, I simply would have seen someone occupying five seats instead of a single seat. I would probably have wondered why she claimed so many seats. There is likely a reason. I think the isthmus condition, the attempt to create a resonance between things, is about imagining that reason, the extending ever outward to entertain the remedying *why*.

6. The Labor of the Isthmus

What if there are no parts? What if all the parts are just landforms waiting for their rightful isthmuses? What if there was once a bridge built, but like the Tacoma Narrows Bridge, it collapsed, sending two landforms into disassociation? It is comforting to think that nearly any two things can cohere—comforting because if they can cohere, then corrupt, bankrupt ideas can unaffix themselves and new linkages can create the latticework upon which all things hinge.

All it takes is one clean gesture, repeated and imprinted, etched and engraved, to attribute a relationship to two disparate things that formerly were not held in relief. These two objects or notions or lines of thought get affixed to one another, and once they do, after enough times they are held in relation; a pathway forms so that they always adhere in our mind (a fixed position of coherence). A series of if/ then or and/with statements form. The disparate notions become embedded in their relationship, and the longer the relationship is given credence, the deeper the entanglement. The deeper the entanglement, the harder it is to estrange these two pathways. They become codified throughways, solidified merely because of their juxtaposition and proximity.

‡ ‡ ‡

Today is January 1, 2019, and the year is already brimming with exigencies. Children list in camps we created for them. Each day while they wait, we enrich our own inaction; we animate all its vile logic. We let the children list. In the last days of 2018, two children, ages seven and eight, both from Guatemala, died in the custody of US border agents tasked with caring for those fallen ill while making the journey between Central America and the United States.

In affixing one thing to another we can make both things holy. By holy, I mean we see both things and then name each object or desire. After we name it, we continue to give it credence by granting it worth—enough to adhere to something else. When we let children list then die, it is a manifestation of our commitment to loosen the ties that bind each of us to each of us. It is a manifestation of our refusal to acknowledge the fact that any two things can cohere, have cohered, and will cohere again.

But if we remember nothing of the middle—the acute thirst, the unrelenting sun at noon, the ache in the lower back, the sores covering someone's feet—then can we create a supple generosity that invites new pathways to form, ones embedded and etched in a long, attenuated love, which has nothing to do with my nation, with your nation, but everything to do with the fact that as long as we are alive, we are bound to each other? And once two things are bound, there is nothing profane about them; they are hallowed. They belong to each other. You can venerate any two things you want to hold in relief, in unity. To do this is to believe in the possible isthmus—to assume, then enact our relational lives. The memory and knowledge of how we have gripped, do grip, and must grip each other may be just outside of our reach, a thin shroud in our memory. But we can turn one more time to face the isthmus, the middle, bearing the acuity of it. The isthmus is fervent. It is ardent, incandescent. The shroud can encase whatever we tell it.

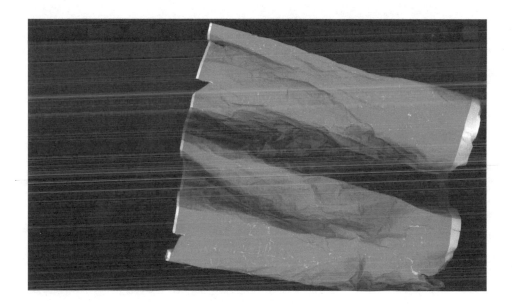

ACKNOWLEDGMENTS

Versions of these poems and essays have appeared in the following journals and publications:

Iowa Review: "my mind makes for me a window then a door"
Baltic Circle Festival Catalog: "seven desire lines one map"
BOMB Magazine: "Nearly Any Two Things Can Cohere"
Gathering Space: "and green waters and green"
Movement Research Performance Journal: "be a bridge over something"
Poem a-Day website: "Shorn, treaded, red"
POETRY: "Mandible Wishbone Solvent"
Poetry Foundation's *Harriet Blog*: "Drift: Against proximal distance from the center"
Propter Nos: "poised in hover hours"
Triple Canopy/Wendy's Subway: "In the checkpoint I was all arms / all face"
Warm Milk: "#221 ½"
Yale Review: "cobalt mirror image 3"

The excerpts that close this book are from the essay "Drift: Against proximal distance from the center" and are portions of a longer essay, some of which emerged through conversations with Sarah Jackson during Telepoetics: Crossed Lines, which was a symposium dedicated to exploring the relationship between telephony and literature. The event was originally scheduled to take place at the Dana Library and Research Centre at the Science Museum in London on May 27, 2020. Due to the impact of COVID-19, however, the event was hosted online. (https://crossedlines.co.uk/telepoetics/).
    Other thoughts mentioned in the "Drift" essay emerged in the days leading up

to a workshop that Brandon Shimoda and I co-taught as part of Pacific Northwest College of Art's low-residency MFA program. Jay Ponteri and I continued thinking about drift together during PNCA's summer 2023 residency. The final version of the full essay appeared in two parts on the Poetry Foundation's *Harriet Blog* in 2021.

"The disc takes shape" was commissioned by Sara Haq in conjunction with her Bethlem Gallery exhibition *metaphysical conundrum*.

Han Kang's *The White Book* and Teju Cole's *Black Paper: Writing in a Dark Time* kept me company while I assembled and ordered this manuscript. Han Kang's words appear as the epigraph to this collection. Teju Cole's logic is, perhaps, embedded elsewhere without my conscious knowledge.

Thank you to the following institutions for supporting the work that appears in this book: the University of Chicago Program in Poetry and Poetics, the Duke University Poetics Working Group, the Finnish Cultural Institute in New York, PUBLICS Helsinki, the Jan Michalski Foundation, the Fiskars Artists in Residence, and the Solomon R. Guggenheim Museum. The Helsinki Central Library Oodi and the Vallila Library Helsinki were my home while I edited and assembled this manuscript.

The pieces in *Mandible Wishbone Solvent* are written in conversation with many artists' work, including Etel Adnan, Howard Smith, Sara Haq, Benjamin Krusling, Miriam Parker, Jean Carla Rodea, Jo Wood-Brown, and Aynsley Vandenbroucke. The following people helped this book come to life: Donika Kelly, Satu Herrala, Tracie Morris, Elina Suoyrjö, Andrew Bourne, Maija Mustonen, mayfield brooks, and Shoshana Olidort. Thank you.

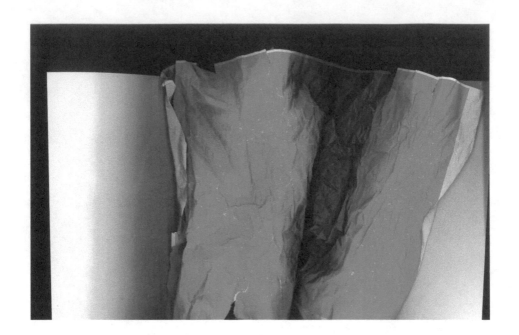

DRIFT: AGAINST PROXIMAL
DISTANCE FROM THE CENTER

"A line of least resistance or to vary or deviate from a set course or adjustment."

In *Merriam-Webster's Collegiate Dictionary*, *drift* the noun and *drift* the verb are defined in a handful of interlocking and overlapping terms. Each time a new meaning is defined, the word *drift* can attenuate or accumulate. The word comes alive through the accumulation of meanings—as the meanings pile up, the image of *drift* crystalizes. A series of images of drift appear—drift in the natural world (an ice floe could drift), drift in our thoughts (the conversation drifted), drift in a geopolitical context (a doomed vessel drifts at sea in the wake of no rescue).

In the litany of meanings, there is also "to move or float smoothly and effortlessly; to move along a line of least resistance." The *resistance* is what I return to resistance as the possible antidote to drift, or maybe the antecedent to drift. Before an object or notion drifts, there is often the act of resisting it. Embedded in the act of drift can be the prior commitment or desire against drifting. Drift extends time on either end—embedded in drift is the knowledge that it, too, once held the center, and that it may not come back to hold it again. We succumb to drift. Or, we can create the conditions in which we always know we will trouble the relationship between the center and the peripheral drift. We succumb to that relationship by design and desire.

In drift's relative distance from its center, we acknowledge the rupture in coherence. Logic has frayed; the object has frayed. In training our eye to the center, drift brings the center's acuity into sharper relief—it brings it into focus. In naming what constitutes the center it also names what is not at the center.

Drift also relates to the excess, the portion that exceeds or defies expectation. It moves at a different pace than the center—and that altered pace defines it as that relative to all else that remains fastened. In this way, drift can become the non sequitur, the "over there." Maybe at first we don't see it or didn't understand its historical relationship to the center, if there ever was one. In the movement of drift, there is a knowledge that that which is now considered drift was once not drift—it held closer to the center. In this way, drift is wrapped up with time. How long does anything need to move away from the center for it to constitute a drift? When do we finally name it *drift*, and what then are the conditions relative to its center?

Can each drift instead also become its own drift-center in a constellation of drift-centers?

The center isn't fraying here, but maybe we are asked to think again about the firmness of the center (which could also be called the *border*, the *plinth*, the *inside*) we have constituted and what it would take to reimagine a new geography and landscape for it.

~~~~~~~

There is still the drift that is "to move or float smoothly and effortlessly." In this acknowledgment, maybe we can soften the firm line between any periphery or border, release the tension a bit between center and otherwise, and assume that things will travel smoothly and effortlessly between center, edge, left of center, and otherwise. The edge will become the center in one frame, and in the next, it could be closer to the edge one more time. Try a third time and again it's back at the edge. But if we stop looking, the animated moment doesn't end; it keeps moving against or toward any expectation. Expecting drift repositions the center and acknowledges that its forcefield is magnetic for this moment but that just outside the frame, there is another, then another field on which to affix new relational drifts.